CW00688047

"These scrupulously inventive translations are indeed love poems for the modern mind, stressing the abiding, unreachable truths and deceptions of intimacy. Petrucci's mastery of linguistic *rubato*, and his profound inwardness with his ancestral Italian, enable Montale's masterpiece to emerge as never before for the reader of English."

PETER BRENNAN

"These are verses of loss and retrieval by means of vivid memories, beloved objects, and intensely felt poetic invention. They are great love poems too, and all the rarer for addressing a wife, not a lover. Petrucci's *Xenia* conveys something new: it emphasises the sequence's quotidian concerns, all its prosaic quirkiness, yet somehow also confirms how unequivocally Montale's greatness transcends the prose-like simplicity of image and tone. Certainly, newcomers to *Xenia* will savour Montale's lasting gift to Mosca, his unforgettable 'little insect' who lives again and forever in these lines."

REBECCA WEST
*Distinguished Service Professor Emerita of Italian Literature,
The University of Chicago*

"In the *Xenia* poems, Montale marries Modernist fragment-ariness with a more conventional desire to memorialise a lost love, often exploiting apparent inconsequence or a seemingly obscure, private sentiment. Mario Petrucci's bold new versions join a distinguished company in helping us to appreciate the strange originality of this work."

MARTYN CRUCEFIX

XENIA

EUGENIO MONTALE
XENIA

A new translation by
Mario Petrucci

PUBLICATIONS
2016

Published by Arc Publications,
Nanholme Mill, Shaw Wood Road
Todmorden OL14 6DA, UK

Original poems copyright © Arnoldo Mondadori Editore S.p.A.,
Milano, 2009
Translation copyright © Mario Petrucci, 2016
Translator's Preface copyright © Mario Petrucci, 2016
Copyright in the present edition © Arc Publications, 2016
978 1910345 53 5 (pbk)
978 1910345 54 2 (hbk)
978 1910345 55 9 (ebook)

Design by Tony Ward

Cover image by Mario Petrucci & Kate Fisher
Cover design by Tony Ward & Ben Styles

This book has been selected to receive financial assistance
from English PEN's PEN Translates programme,
supported by Arts Council England. PEN exists to promote
literature and our understanding of it, to uphold writers'
freedoms around the world, to campaign against the
persecution and imprisonment of writers for stating their
views, and to promote the friendly co-operation of writers
and the free exchange of ideas.
www.englishpen.org

'Arc Classics:
New Translations of Great Poets of the Past'
Series Editor: Jean Boase-Beier

TRANSLATOR'S ACKNOWLEDGEMENTS

My thanks go to Peter Brennan and Martyn Crucefix for their considered comments, to Marisha Horsman for such frequent surrendering to the role of sounding board, and to Romilda Mormile for her generous assistance with some of the finer points of Italian.

The early (1966, 1968, 1970) Italian editions of *Xenia* carry fascinating differences, among themselves as well as relative to more modern versions of the source text (*Xenia* was later subsumed into the volume *Satura* (1971), but only after several less conspicuous incarnations). In accessing and investigating these rare publications, I was much aided by Gabriele Rossini (Centro per gli studi sulla tradizione manoscritta di autori moderni e contemporanei dell'Università di Pavia), Alessandra Mariani (Biblioteca Nazionale Centrale di Roma), Caterina Silva (Fondazione Museo Bodoniano, Parma) and Maria Riccobono (Eugenio Montale Library, Italian Cultural Institute, London).

The Italian texts for *Xenia* presented in subsequent (including bilingual) editions of Montale also often disagree (though, usually, merely in certain details). I therefore compared the many published works available to me when compiling the Italian for this book, in an attempt to pinpoint the discrepancies and eliminate the more obvious errors. I shall have to thank those sources collectively, though I must say that the 2009 Mondadori edition of *Satura* (edited by R. Castellana) and *L'opera in versi (I millenni)* from Einaudi (1980) became especially valuable and turned out to be very close indeed to the form of the original I eventually chose.

Mario Petrucci

CONTENTS

*"… poetry has always died
and is ever revived from its ashes."*

EUGENIO MONTALE

If Eugenio Montale (in spite of his 1975 Nobel Prize, Robert Lowell's extraordinary *Imitations*, and a full-scale apotheosis at the hands of F. R. Leavis) is still insufficiently read in Britain, it's perhaps to do with the fact that here "those sweet wines / just aren't in fashion" (*Xenia II*, 8). This is a considerable shame because, as Jeremy Reed so aptly puts it, "Montale's free but controlled verse fits the shape of the century in which it is written." I'd go further and say that his verse helped *define* that shape.

Montale's *Xenia* came in profound response to the death, in 1963, of his wife Drusilla Tanzi. It's been likened to Thomas Hardy's *Poems of 1912-13* (from *Satires of Circumstance*) – the much-acclaimed verse memorial to Emma, Hardy's first wife – which Montale himself admired as "one of the summits of modern poetry". Kate Hughes, introducing her *Xenia and Motets* (Agenda Editions, 1980), considered *Xenia* "arguably Montale's highest achievement"; G. Singh (*Agenda* magazine, 1971/2) believed that "In terms of technique, style and diction... there is no parallel in Italian poetry"; and Leavis, having contemplated the work as somehow characteristically English, then wryly added: "But I must confess... we have nothing like it in English." Leavis's confession would have conveyed a whiff of truism to Lowell, who tells us (in *Imitations*) that, for important poems in other tongues, "Nothing like them exists in English, for the excellence of a poet depends on the unique opportunities of his native language." Even so, *Xenia* still unveils, for me, even in translation, Montale's most trenchant testimony to what he describes (when referring to the source of "all real poetry") as "an internal void provisionally filled by the achievement of expression" (from *Poet in Our Time*, 1976, translated by Alastair Hamilton).

In *Xenia*, therefore, we encounter Montale in a singular

mood, which may help to explain why critics, Leavis included, have considered it a landmark in his oeuvre. Here, Montale's evasive, largely depersonalised "tu" – in the form of his emblematic, transcendental female character, Clizia – is finally reified in the person of Drusilla, his 'Mosca', a woman so short-sighted that she (reputedly) once bumped into a mirror and apologised to her reflection. A dominant star in Montale's constellation of muses, Clizia has come to be associated with Irma Brandeis, a protagonist he presents in shrouds and evocative mists; but *Xenia* delivers a kind of clarification for the allusive poet, a consummating condensation of his *donna fantasma*, his Beatrice, into the lived-with actuality of his wife. There is such decisive contrast with his previous craft, the concentrated imagery giving way to a simplicity of frank expression. Rather than mining the universal to capture the particular, he now releases quotidian objects – particular, mourned-over objects – into the universal. He intensifies the intimacy merely suggested in his previous books, doing so through a distinctively colloquial airing of life's minutiae that, in spite of its impromptu feel, forgets nothing of his trademark detachment and deliberation. The familiarities of a shared life are allowed to brim but never to spill over, as they might under less dextrous or more assertive hands, into sentimentality. Those details, things as things *in* themselves, contain the emotion. Around housebound bric-à-brac and household oddments – a telephone bill, old books, his (as he elsewhere puts it) "totem" of a rusty shoehorn – Montale constructs a humble reliquary of loss. And yet, that tatty bible with which he opens *Xenia I* (a fitting omen for the flood closing *Xenia II*) poignantly symbolises his desire to erect from an individual grief and its memorabilia, albeit in an underplayed manner, a reverential monument. The ageing poet, inventorying the inundated rag-and-bone shop of his heart, nevertheless does so with one eye on the museum and public square. With so much going on, then, it's hardly surprising that academic and translator alike should gravitate towards this work.

Turning to prosody, it's interesting to note that *Xenia*, according to at least one commentary, has been thought to consist of prose fragments. That it does *not* is evidenced by far more than its line breaks. In fact, the overall demeanour of *Xenia* has something of the epigram about it. Singh has revealed that Montale had *Xenien* – the Goethe-Schiller epigrams – "in mind" when choosing his own title. Moreover, there are plausible resemblances, emphasised by Italian-American author F. L. Gardaphe, between Montale's *Xenia* and the epigrams of Martial, who also composed 'Xenia': for instance, their conversational yet dispassionate irony, the effective use of repetition, their shared wittiness around the naming of wines, the symbolising cataloguing of objects. But the case for *Xenia* as poetry of a high order – rather than heightened prose – goes way beyond that. Achieving what Leavis described as "rightness (that is, decisive inevitability) in relation to rhythm and structure", Montale's understated poetic musicality becomes less avoidable, perhaps, when the poems are read out loud. In a loose mix of free and more formal measures, his canny consonantal chimes and crisp, unprosaic stitching of vowels grow clearer, the latter exploiting to the full the twill-like texturing of running agreements in Italian. However, the soft, easy sonority of his mother tongue can tax the thesaurus, as much as the ear, of the English translator. Montale continually evades the saccharine; but the vowel-led tendency to sweetness inherent in Italian doesn't always travel well. Nevertheless, I've attempted to preserve something of the subtlety, that binding quality, of his music. In rendering "dolcezza e orrore in una sola musica" as "honey and horror in the one harmony" (*Xenia II*, 4), I strive to demonstrate not my skill as a translator so much as the suppleness and versatility of English.

I should add that I skirted, initially, the Matterhorn of Montale commentaries, not wishing to commence *Xenia* in the boa grip of academic conclusions or with that pressing sense of an author's sanctified objectives. This might seem cavalier, even heretical, with someone as elusive and allusive as Montale can be; but it paid the language, as well as the poet, a different sort of respect. It allowed a fresh and unencumbered approach, one that (for all its dangers) facilitated a certain freedom to express and reinterpret the spirit of the verse. I was able to come to textual insights in my own way rather than second-hand. For similar reasons, I conducted the bulk of my study of existing translations only at the editing-revising stage. I could thereby enjoy – as my own – such sonic felicities (in its specific context) as "gawky". This particular eureka wasn't long-lived (I later found that William Arrowsmith had beaten me to it); but it typifies the rich engagement I wanted my *Xenia* to be imbued with. My inclination for an "unencumbered approach" carried over into my decision not to supply footnotes to the poems. Some facts or interpretations I might have noted more formally have already been touched upon in this preface and, in any case, I saw scant value in replicating what has been compiled in concise and readable form elsewhere (as in Arrowsmith's 1998 *Satura*, or Singh's 1976 *Eugenio Montale: New Poems*).

So, for anyone seeking here the purities of literalism, or some poetic device tuned to Montale's precise intentions gleaned through in-depth investigative scholarship, disappointment awaits. Indeed, with my occasional taking of poetic liberties, this *Xenia* could be dubbed (to adapt Dryden's terminology) 'fastidious imitation'. Within this general thrust, I felt that Montale's music, his (as I put it earlier) "giving way to a simplicity of frank expression", were not to be played too simplistically. As one of the last few of the statuesque High Modernists, the core of his style – even in *Xenia* – has much to do with a subtle combination of nuance, suggestiveness and poise that serves to complicate and pluralise significance. This hybrid characteristic is washed out, crucially, from any translation seeking to overemphasise the plain or 'essential' meaning of his lines. Where I have most departed, then, from most other translations is in occasionally 'turning up the contrast', as it were, on ambiguity and strangeness where I discerned them or – to be candid – most desired to read them in. If, in bringing those qualities closer to the finished surface, some passages have (to some tastes) become a little too grainy: *mea culpa*. It was a risk, an imposition I consciously undertook in order to capitalise, inside English, on Montale's hard-won singularity.

߯

I can't say I've any clear idea what I was doing on that September late Saturday that Montale died. If any report did filter through the English media on the Sunday, I doubt I would have registered it. As a young secondary school teacher, I was probably planning the provision of physics lessons, my mind further from poetry than I could ever now conceive. Montale's name meant little to me; nor did I know, steeped in my particular form of provinciality, that Leavis had already elevated him to the status of one "as truly sophisticated as a major artist can be." In some ways, I was then (maybe still am) a symptom of what Montale addresses at the end of *Xenia* via his Florentine ark of artefacts overwhelmed in the calamitous flood of 1966. Orchestrated with great care, those objects resurface as a metaphor for a loss that is, as Arrowsmith suggests in his notes to the poem, "both personal and historical". Not only is Montale's private past with Mosca submerged but also a high literary culture whose ruination is (Arrowsmith again) "wrought by industrialization, and the impact of mass society, mass culture", as if "the flood had swept away a part of the mind of Europe". Immersed in my time, in its High Mass of commercialism, I – along with many others – was mindless of that.

Given my impression that Montale, along with European poetry in general, is under-read in Britain, it would seem the mindlessness continues. I doubt I'll ever be able to recite any substantial chunk of *Xenia* from memory, let alone – as Montale and Leavis were capable of doing (albeit in relays) when they met in Milan – the whole of Valéry's *Le Cimetière Marin*. I could argue that I, like most of my generation, have more pressing, more modern priorities; alternatively, I might consider how far our culture displays an erosion of what Hardy calls (in *Late Lyrics and Earlier*, 1922) "high thinking", wherein "we seem threatened with a new Dark Age" (thoughts that provide another correspondence between Hardy and Montale). At my age, I daren't – not quite, not yet – pass equivalent judgement on my Age; but I do propose that a quarter-century ought to be enough for an individual, if not his generation, to offer redress. With this belated *Xenia*, I hope to have gone some small way towards redeeming my personal omission.

Mario Petrucci
October 2006

NOTES

This translation and preface were composed primarily in 2006, as dated above, twenty-five years after Montale's death. I'm delighted that a decade's wait for publication has not only led to their editorial maturation but has also brought them into alignment with the fiftieth anniversary of Montale's 1966 private edition of *Xenia* (whose fifty copies contained part I of the sequence only).

The quotations from Leavis are taken from his *Xenia* essay, as published in *Eugenio Montale: New Poems* (translated by G. Singh, Chatto & Windus, 1976). I felt I should identify my source clearly here, as Leavis is so prominent in my discussions.

In addition, on the very few occasions I quote from Montale's writings without specifying the translator, it should be understood that those are my own renderings into English.

SELECTED BIBLIOGRAPHY
(for the Italian text)

EARLY [RARE] ITALIAN SOURCES FOR *XENIA*
Eugenio Montale, *Xenia (1964-1966)*, San Severino Marche: Bellabarba (1966).
Eugenio Montale, *Xenia*, Editiones Dominicae (Verona, 1968).
Eugenio Montale, *Xenia*, Editiones Dominicae (Verona, 1970).

LATER ITALIAN SOURCES FOR *XENIA*
Eugenio Montale, *Satura: 1962-1970*, Arnoldo Mondadori Editore (Italy, 1971).
Eugenio Montale [ed. G. Singh], *Montale: Selected Poems*, Manchester University Press (Manchester, 1975).
Eugenio Montale [eds. R. Bettarini & G. Contini], *L'opera in versi (I millenni)*, Einaudi (Turin, 1980).
Eugenio Montale [ed. R. Castellana], *Satura*, Oscar poesia del Novecento, Mondadori (Milan, 2009).

BILINGUAL
Kate Hughes, *Xenia and Motets*, Agenda Editions (London, 1980).
Jeremy Reed, *The Coastguard's House*, Bloodaxe Books (Newcastle upon Tyne, 1990).
William Arrowsmith, *Satura: 1962-1970*, Norton (New York / London, 1998).

XENIA I

1

Caro piccolo insetto
che chiamavano mosca non so perché,
stasera quasi al buio
mentre leggevo il Deuteroisaia
sei ricomparsa accanto a me,
ma non avevi occhiali,
non potevi vedermi
né potevo io senza quel luccichìo
riconoscere te nella foschia.

1

Dear little insect
they called – I don't know why – *fly*,
this evening on the brink of dark
while I was reading Deutero-Isaiah
you recomposed, right here, beside:
but had no glasses
couldn't see me
nor could I, without their spark,
tell you from murk.

2

Senza occhiali né antenne,
povero insetto che ali
avevi solo nella fantasia,
una bibbia sfasciata ed anche poco
attendibile, il nero della notte,
un lampo, un tuono e poi
neppure la tempesta. Forse che
te n'eri andata così presto senza
parlare? Ma è ridicolo
pensare che tu avessi ancora labbra.

2

No glasses, nor antennae,
poor insect – such wings
you possessed only in fantasy –
a bible broken and much less
believable, this night-blackness,
a flash, a clap and then
no – not even the squall. Perhaps
you never left so soon without
speaking? Though it's laughable
to consider you still had lips.

3

Al Saint James di Parigi dovrò chiedere
una camera 'singola'. (Non amano
i clienti spaiati). E così pure
nella falsa Bisanzio del tuo albergo
veneziano; per poi cercare subito
lo sgabuzzino delle telefoniste,
le tue amiche di sempre; e ripartire,
esaurita la carica meccanica,
il desiderio di riaverti, fosse
pure in un solo gesto o un'abitudine.

3

At the Saint James, Paris, I'll request
a *single* room. (No love lost there
for the uncoupled client). So, too,
in the mock Byzantium of your
Venetian hotel; then quick on the scent
of those friends of yours in their
switchboard hutch; only to start
again, my clockwork charge all spent,
with that longing to have you back if
only in some gesture, or knack.

4

Avevamo studiato per l'aldilà
un fischio, un segno di riconoscimento.
Mi provo a modularlo nella speranza
che tutti siamo già morti senza saperlo.

4

Together, for the hereafter, we contrived
a whistle – our means of recognition.
I'm going deep in its perfection, in the hope
we're already dead, without knowing.

5

Non ho mai capito se io fossi
il tuo cane fedele e incimurrito
o tu lo fossi per me.
Per gli altri no, eri un insetto miope
smarrito nel blabla
dell'alta società. Erano ingenui
quei furbi e non sapevano
di essere loro il tuo zimbello:
di esser visti anche al buio e smascherati
da un tuo senso infallibile, dal tuo
radar di pipistrello.

5

I never did understand whether
I was your dog, faithful, purblind –
or vice versa. To others, no,
you were some myopic insect
mislaid among the *blah-blahs*
of high intelligentsia. Artless
they were, sly fools, not to guess
they were your decoy: so clear
even in the dark, unmasked
by that unfailing sense, by your
moth-eating radar.

6

Non hai pensato mai di lasciar traccia
di te scrivendo prosa o versi. E fu
il tuo incanto – e dopo la mia nausea di me.
Fu pure il mio terrore: di esser poi
ricacciato da te nel gracidante
limo dei neòteroi.

6

You never thought to leave
your mark, either prose or verse. Right
there – your charm – my self-induced nausea
came later. My terror, too: to be at last
driven back by you into that croaksome
mire of the modernists.

7

Pietà di sé, infinita pena e angoscia
di chi adora il *quaggiù* e spera e dispera
di un altro... (Chi osa dire un altro mondo?).

.   .   .

«Strana pietà...» (Azucena, atto secondo).

7

Self-pity, unlimited pain and hurt
for the *down-here* devotee hoping, against hope,
for another... (Who'd dare speak another world?).

.   .   .   .   .

Such strange pity... (Azucena, second act).

8

La tua parola così stenta e imprudente
resta la sola di cui mi appago.
Ma è mutato l'accento, altro il colore.
Mi abituerò a sentirti o a decifrarti
nel ticchettìo della telescrivente,
nel volubile fumo dei miei sigari
di Brissago.

8

Your word – so hesitant, so rash –
still my sole satisfaction. But the accent
has altered; the tenor too. I'll have to
accustom myself: hear, decipher,
you in the telex ticking over,
in this fickle smoulder
of Brissago cigar.

9

Ascoltare era il solo tuo modo di vedere.
Il conto del telefono s'è ridotto a ben poco.

9

Listening was your sole means of seeing.
The telephone bill is reduced to nothing.

10

«Pregava?». «Sì, pregava Sant'Antonio
perché fa ritrovare
gli ombrelli smarriti e altri oggetti
del guardaroba di Sant'Ermete».
«Per questo solo?». «Anche per i suoi morti
e per me».
       «È sufficiente» disse il prete.

10

And prayer? Yes, to Saint Anthony
for the salvation
of waif-brollies and inanimate bodies
from the understairs of sainted Hermes.
Is that it? For her dead too
and for me.
                That'll do, the priest declared.

11

Ricordare il tuo pianto (il mio era doppio)
non vale a spenger lo scoppio delle tue risate.
Erano come l'anticipo di un tuo privato
Giudizio Universale, mai accaduto purtroppo.

11

To remember such tears (mine were double)
does little to muffle your gunshot laugh.
They were like the trailer for your personal
Apocalypse, a non-event. Too much?

12

La primavera sbuca col suo passo di talpa.
Non ti sentirò più parlare di antibiotici
velenosi, del chiodo del tuo femore,
dei beni di fortuna che t'ha un occhiuto omissis
spennacchiati.

La primavera avanza con le sue nebbie grasse,
con le sue luci lunghe, le sue ore insopportabili.
Non ti sentirò più lottare col rigurgito
del tempo, dei fantasmi, dei problemi logistici
dell'Estate.

12

Springtime barrels along at mole-pace.
I'll not hear your talk of antibiotics and their
venoms, of the six-incher through your femur,
of your fortune read by sharp-eyed ~~omission~~
then plucked bare.

Springtime advances its greasy fogs,
its longsuffering light, its intolerable *tock-tick*.
I'll no longer hear you wrestle that reflux
of time, those ghouls, the awful logistics
of summer.

13

Tuo fratello morì giovane; tu eri
la bimba scarruffata che mi guarda
'in posa' nell'ovale di un ritratto.
Scrisse musiche inedite, inaudite,
oggi sepolte in un baule o andate
al màcero. Forse le riinventa
qualcuno inconsapevole, se ciò ch'è scritto è scritto.
L'amavo senza averlo conosciuto.
Fuori di te nessuno lo ricordava.
Non ho fatto ricerche: ora è inutile.
Dopo di te sono rimasto il solo
per cui egli è esistito. Ma è possibile,
lo sai, amare un'ombra, ombre noi stessi.

13

Your brother died early; you were
that urchin watching over me
posing as the oval of a picture.
His music – unpublished, unsung,
now sepulchred in a trunk or pulped
in the vat. Perhaps it's being reinvented,
recomposed unawares, if what is written stays written.
I loved him without knowing him.
Beyond you, none remembered him.
I didn't probe: and now it's pointless.
After you, I'm the only soul
for whom he existed. Though I guess we're
permitted to love the shade, being shade ourselves.

14

Dicono che la mia
sia una poesia d'inappartenenza.
Ma s'era tua era di qualcuno:
di te che non sei più forma, ma essenza.
Dicono che la poesia al suo culmine
magnifica il Tutto in fuga,
negano che la testuggine
sia più veloce del fulmine.
Tu sola sapevi che il moto
non è diverso dalla stasi,
che il vuoto è il pieno e il sereno
è la più diffusa delle nubi.
Così meglio intendo il tuo lungo viaggio
imprigionata tra le bende e i gessi.
Eppure non mi dà riposo
sapere che in uno o in due noi siamo una sola cosa.

14

They consider mine
a poetry of unbelonging.
But if it was yours, it was somebody's:
of you – no longer formed, but essential.
They consider poetry at its zenith
a Magnificat, a fugue to All,
denying that the turtle
be swifter than the bolt.
You alone knew the jolt
no different from stasis,
that the void is fullness, the blue
thinnest cloud. So I better
understand your long journey
incarcerated in bandage and plaster.
Yet I've no peace in knowing that
we, taken singly or together, make one matter.

XENIA II

1

La morte non ti riguardava.
Anche i tuoi cani erano morti, anche
il medico dei pazzi detto lo zio demente,
anche tua madre e la sua 'specialità'
di riso e rane, trionfo meneghino;
e anche tuo padre che da una minieffigie
mi sorveglia dal muro sera e mattina.
Malgrado ciò la morte non ti riguardava.

Ai funerali dovevo andare io,
nascosto in un tassì, restandone lontano
per evitare lacrime e fastidi. E neppure
t'importava la vita e le sue fiere
di vanità e ingordige e tanto meno le
cancrene universali che trasformano
gli uomini in lupi.

Una tabula rasa; se non fosse
che un punto c'era, per me incomprensibile,
e questo punto *ti riguardava*.

1

Death wouldn't look you over.
Even though your dogs were dead, even
that psychiatrist known as Uncle Lunatic,
even your own mother with her 'specialty'
of frog risotto (that flash in the pan from Milan);
and even your father who, from his mini-grotto
on the wall, keeps round-the-clock surveillance.
And still death overlooked you.

It was me attending funerals,
skulking in a cab, standing far off
to avoid the tedium of tears. Not even
life struck you with its frenzied
vanity, its hungers, and even less those
ubiquitous cankers – transformers
of humans into wolves.

A clean copybook, then; if it weren't
for the one blot, incomprehensible to me,
and how *you looked* to this blot.

2

Spesso ti ricordavi (io poco) del signor Cap.
«L'ho visto nel torpedone, a Ischia, appena due volte.
È un avvocato di Klagenfurt, quello che manda gli auguri.
Doveva venirci a trovare».

E infine è venuto, gli dico tutto, resta imbambolato,
pare che sia una catastrofe anche per lui. Tace a lungo,
farfuglia, s'alza rigido e s'inchina. Conferma
che manderà gli auguri.
                          È strano che a comprenderti
siano riuscite solo persone inverosimili.
Il dottor Cap! Basta il nome. E Celia? Che n'è accaduto?

2

Often, you'd recall (I, rarely) Herr Kap.
That barrister in Klagenfurt. The one who sends his best…
I saw him on the bus, in Ischia, maybe twice?
He meant to visit us.

And at last he comes, I tell him everything, he's punch-
drunk with it, as if it were his disaster too. A hush
before he slurs a few words, gets up, stiffly, bows.
Confirms he'll send his best.
                              Peculiar, how
only peculiar people managed to know you.
Doktor Kap! That *name.* And Celia? How did she end up?

3

L'abbiamo rimpianto a lungo l'infilascarpe,
il cornetto di latta arrugginito ch'era
sempre con noi. Pareva un'indecenza portare
tra i similori e gli stucchi un tale orrore.
Dev'essere al Danieli che ho scordato
di riporlo in valigia o nel sacchetto.
Hedia la cameriera lo buttò certo
nel Canalazzo. E come avrei potuto
scrivere che cercassero quel pezzaccio di latta?
C'era un prestigio (il nostro) da salvare
e Hedia, la fedele, l'aveva fatto.

3

For ages we mourned it – that little
shoehorn of rusty tin we'd take along
wherever we went. Such a thing seemed
obscene amid the ormolu and ornamentation.
It had to be at the Danieli that I forgot
to return it to my suitcase, or holdall.
I'm sure Hedia, the cleaner, threw it in
the Grand Canal. How would I have written,
asking them to look for that lump of tin?
A certain status (ours) was on the line
and Hedia, old faithful, salvaged it.

4

Con astuzia,
uscendo dalle fauci di Mongibello
o da dentiere di ghiaccio
rivelavi incredibili agnizioni.

Se ne avvide Mangàno, il buon cerusico,
quando, disoccultato, fu il randello
delle camicie nere e ne sorrise.

Così eri: anche sul ciglio del crepaccio
dolcezza e orrore in una sola musica.

4

Fly,
emerging from Etna's craw
or from its glacial dentition
you divined uncanny connections.

Beni, the good butcher, got wind of it
when exposed as erstwhile iron hand
of the Blackshirts, and returned a smile.

That's you: even on the brow of the fissure –
honey and horror in the one harmony.

5

Ho sceso, dandoti il braccio, almeno un milione di scale
e ora che non ci sei è il vuoto ad ogni gradino.
Anche così è stato breve il nostro lungo viaggio.
Il mio dura tuttora, né più mi occorrono
le coincidenze, le prenotazioni,
le trappole, gli scorni di chi crede
che la realtà sia quella che si vede.

Ho sceso milioni di scale dandoti il braccio
non già perché con quattr'occhi forse si vede di più.
Con te le ho scese perché sapevo che di noi due
le sole vere pupille, sebbene tanto offuscate,
erano le tue.

5

I've descended, your arm in mine, a million stairs at least
and now that you're gone there's the void at every step.
Even so, our long journey – it's been brief.
Mine goes on, still, though I've no further need
for connections, reservations,
the snares, the pillory of whoever believes
that reality is the one you see.

I've descended millions of stairways arm in arm
not – of course – because four eyes may see more.
I went down them, with you, because I knew that between
we two the favoured, the true, pupils (though quite dim)
were yours.

6

Il vinattiere ti versava un poco
d'Inferno. E tu, atterrita: «Devo berlo? Non basta
esserci stati dentro a lento fuoco?».

6

The wine pedlar poured you a spot
of Inferno. And you, figurine of terror: *Must I? Isn't it out
of order to have already been – right in it, on a low heat?*

7

«Non sono mai stato certo di essere al mondo».
«Bella scoperta, m'hai risposto, e io?».
«Oh il mondo tu l'hai mordicchiato, se anche
in dosi omeopatiche. Ma io…».

7

"I've never been sure I was of this world."
Some discovery – you've answered me. And what of myself?
"Oh you've gnawed from its edges, if only
in homeopathic doses. While I…"

8

«E il Paradiso? Esiste un paradiso?».
«Credo di sì, signora, ma i vini dolci
non li vuol più nessuno».

8

And Paradiso? Might there be some paradise?
"I reckon so, ma'am. Though those sweet wines
just aren't in fashion."

9

Le monache e le vedove, mortifere
maleodoranti prefiche,
non osavi guardarle. Lui stesso che ha mille occhi,
li distoglie da loro, n'eri certa.
L'onniveggente, lui… perché tu, giudiziosa,
dio non lo nominavi neppure con la minuscola.

9

The nuns, the dowagers, those ruinous
malodorous freelance mourners –
you shrunk from looking. He of a thousand eyes
averts them from them, you were certain of it.
The panoptic one... *him*. For you, so circumspect,
would never name-drop god, not even in a tiny font.

10

Dopo lunghe ricerche
ti trovai in un bar dell'Avenida
da Liberdade; non sapevi un'acca
di portoghese o meglio una parola
sola: Madeira. E venne il bicchierino
con un contorno di aragostine.

La sera fui paragonato ai massimi
lusitani dai nomi impronunciabili
e al Carducci in aggiunta.
Per nulla impressionata io ti vedevo piangere
dal ridere nascosta in una folla
forse annoiata ma compunta.

10

After much searching
I found you in a bar on the Avenida
da Liberdade; you didn't have an aitch
of Portuguese, or better to say you'd only
one word: *Madeira*. And the wineglass came
with scampi on the side.

That evening I was compared to supreme
Lusitanians with unpronounceable names
and to Carducci, no less.
I saw you weeping, quite unimpressed,
with laughter, deep in a crowd –
bored perhaps, but contrite.

11

Riemersa da un'infinità di tempo
Celia la filippina ha telefonato
per aver tue notizie. Credo stia bene, dico,
forse meglio di prima. «Come, crede?
Non c'è più?». Forse più di prima, ma...
Celia, cerchi d'intendere...
                           Di là dal filo,
da Manila o da altra
parola dell'atlante una balbuzie
impediva anche lei. E riagganciò di scatto.

11

Resurfacing from an infinity of time
Celia (the Filipina) telephoned
for news of you. I say – She's fine, I think.
Better than before maybe. *How come, 'You think'?*
Isn't she there any more? Perhaps more so, but…
Celia, try to understand…
                    Down that line,
from Manila or from some other
atlas-name, a stammer
hampered her too. She rang off. Pronto.

12

I falchi
sempre troppo lontani dal tuo sguardo
raramente li hai visti davvicino.
Uno a Étretat che sorvegliava i goffi
voli dei suoi bambini.
Due altri in Grecia, sulla via di Delfi,
una zuffa di piume soffici, due becchi giovani
arditi e inoffensivi.

Ti piaceva la vita fatta a pezzi,
quella che rompe dal suo insopportabile
ordito.

12

Hawks –
always beyond your scope,
rarely did you see them up close.
One, at Étretat, keeping an eye on the
gawky flight of its fledglings.
Two others, in Greece, on the road to Delphi –
a fracas of soft feathers, two juvenile beaks
fierce and inoffensive.

You liked life through a shredder –
the type breaking through its intolerable
tissue.

13

Ho appeso nella mia stanza il dagherròtipo
di tuo padre bambino: ha più di un secolo.
In mancanza del mio, così confuso,
cerco di ricostruire, ma invano, il tuo pedigree.
Non siamo stati cavalli, i dati dei nostri ascendenti
non sono negli almanacchi. Coloro che hanno presunto
di saperne non erano essi stessi esistenti,
né noi per loro. E allora? Eppure resta
che qualcosa è accaduto, forse un niente
che è tutto.

13

In my room I've put up the daguerreotype
of your father as a child: over a hundred years old.
Lacking any pedigree of my own (so addled)
I vainly attempt to reconstruct yours.
We haven't been horses; the data for our forbears
aren't in the breed registry. Those who've presumed
to know them weren't in existence themselves,
nor were we for them. What then? Yet it remains
that something befell us – perhaps a nothing
that is all there is.

14

L'alluvione ha sommerso il pack dei mobili,
delle carte, dei quadri che stipavano
un sotterraneo chiuso a doppio lucchetto.
Forse hanno ciecamente lottato i marocchini
rossi, le sterminate dediche di Du Bos,
il timbro a ceralacca con la barba di Ezra,
il Valéry di Alain, l'originale
dei Canti Orfici – e poi qualche pennello
da barba, mille cianfrusaglie e tutte
le musiche di tuo fratello Silvio.
Dieci, dodici giorni sotto un'atroce morsura
di nafta e sterco. Certo hanno sofferto
tanto prima di perdere la loro identità.
Anch'io sono incrostato fino al collo se il mio
stato civile fu dubbio fin dall'inizio.
Non torba m'ha assediato, ma gli eventi
di una realtà incredibile e mai creduta.
Di fronte ad essi il mio coraggio fu il primo
dei tuoi prestiti e forse non l'hai saputo.

14

Drowned, in alluvium, the menagerie of furniture,
the documents, the pictures penned in
a basement doubly barred and bolted.
Perhaps they turned, unseeing, on one another,
the red Moroccan tomes, Du Bos's boundless dedications,
the sealing-wax stamped with Ezra's beard,
Alain's Valéry, that first edition
of *Orphic Songs* – along with a few
shaving brushes, a thousand curios and all
the compositions of your brother Silvio.
Ten, twelve days beneath a stinging atrocity
of naphtha and shit. Surely, they suffered
greatly before losing their identity.
I'm encrusted to the collar too – if my
civilised state was doubtful from the start.
It's not rot that has me under siege, but the events
of a reality at odds with belief, and never believed.
My bravery, before these, was chief among all
my debts to you – maybe you didn't know that.

EUGENIO MONTALE (1896-1981) is one of Italy's most fa-
mous poets and a grandmaster of modernist poetry. From
his early, groundbreaking *Ossi di seppia* (1925) to his late
masterpiece *Satura* (1971), his was a voice that remained
both distinctive and original, representing something
of a watershed for Italian poetics. He was an Anglophile
much influenced by (among others) T. S. Eliot and G. M.
Hopkins, and was instrumental in presenting English-
speaking poets to Italian readers through his translations
of such luminaries as Shakespeare, Eliot, Yeats and Emily
Dickinson. Robert Lowell, who had "long been amazed by
Montale", featured him prominently in *Imitations* (1961).
Winner of the 1975 Nobel Prize for Literature, Montale
was an anti-fascist and a Senator in the Italian Parliament.
His early love of music endured throughout his private
and professional life, and he served as music critic as well
as literary editor for the *Corriere della Sera*.

MARIO PETRUCCI is an ecologist, physicist and prize-win-
ning poet, renowned for combining innovation and lin-
guistic excitement with profound humanity. He is the only
poet to have held residencies at the Imperial War Museum
and with BBC Radio 3. Described as "Heartfelt, ambitious
and alive" (*The Daily Telegraph*), his Arvon-winning *Heavy
Water: a poem for Chernobyl* (Enitharmon, 2004) led to an in-
ternationally acclaimed poetry film (Seventh Art Produc-
tions). Petrucci's vast 3D poetry soundscape, *Tales from the
Bridge*, was a centrepiece of London's Cultural Olympiad
and was shortlisted for the 2012 Ted Hughes Award. His
published and forthcoming translation projects include:
Catullus, Sappho ("utterly compelling", *Daily Mail*), Pablo
Neruda, and the Persian mediaeval poet Hafez.
www.mariopetrucci.com

ARC PUBLICATIONS
publishes translated poetry in bilingual editions
in these series:

ARC TRANSLATIONS
Series Editor Jean Boase-Beier

'VISIBLE POETS'
Series Editor Jean Boase-Beier

ARC CLASSICS:
NEW TRANSLATIONS OF GREAT POETS OF THE PAST
Series Editor Jean Boase-Beier

ARC ANTHOLOGIES IN TRANSLATION
Series Editor Jean Boase-Beier

NEW VOICES FROM EUROPE & BEYOND
(anthologies)
Series Editor Alexandra Büchler

Details of these series can be found on the
Arc Publications website at
arcpublications.co.uk

Lightning Source UK Ltd.
Milton Keynes UK
UKHW010647221220
375698UK00001B/65